—

THE
RAINFOREST

SCORECARD

A Practical Framework
for Growing Innovation Potential

—

PUBLISHED BY REGENWALD
LOS ALTOS, CALIFORNIA, U.S.A.

Cover and book design by Bill Rogers

Printed in the United States of America

ISBN-13: 978-0-9882746-2-4

Library of Congress Control Number: 2015931268

Edition 1.0 (January 2015)

 REGENWALD®

AKNOWLEDGEMENTS

No text such as this *Rainforest Scorecard* comes into the world alone. It is the result of countless conversations, emails, dialogues, discussions, and shared inquiry, on the part of many, many people. It is in fact an ongoing and continuously growing dialogue. Listing everyone who contributed to the making of this little book, or who will contribute to its evolution, would be an impossible task. Still, at the risk of leaving out someone who merits recognition, it is worth trying to acknowledge some of those who have been—and will continue to be —a part of making this work come into being. In that spirit, we appreciate and thank: Victor Hwang, Greg Horowitt, Mark Newburg, Joe Sterling, Jason Steiner, Tom Guevara, Ade Mabogunje, Scott Gillespie, Janet Crawford.

FOREWORD
by Victor W. Hwang

Big things often come in little packages. You are holding a book that, while small in size, is colossal in potential impact. This *Rainforest Scorecard* is the world's first comprehensive scientific measurement tool for growing innovative, entrepreneurial ecosystems. Its authors, Henry Doss and Alistair Brett, have made a profound gift to the world.

Why does the world need such a tool? The game has changed. The age of industrialization has passed, and the world has entered the age of knowledge. What worked in the past will not work so well in the future. And most of the world, riding the momentum of its past, is facing a pivotal moment—will it be able to adapt to the new economic game?

The new game is based on innovation. And innovation is basically the counterpoint to production. Whereas production calls for predictability, innovation allows for mistakes and failures. Whereas production calls for efficiency, innovation seeks experimentation. Whereas production often calls for cold-blooded competition, innovation thrives on positive-sum collaboration among diverse strangers.

To foster innovation, therefore, leaders need new levers. We can see the outlines of a new model based on the nurturing of entire innovative ecosystems, not just the strength of input factors. Such ecosystems, at a micro level, depend on interactions among human beings. Those patterns of interactions are what we call culture. *Culture, therefore, is a lever for economic growth.* Think about that statement. It is revolutionary.

So where can we learn how to build such ecosystems? The greatest ecosystem of our time happens to be Silicon Valley. And the profound, ironic lesson of Silicon Valley is that it is not actually a place at all. It's a state of mind. Values such as diversity, connectivity, trust, collaboration, experimentation, and passion—they are the invisible engine that powers the Valley's economy.

Fortunately for us, states of mind are free. The values of Silicon Valley are universal. At a deep level, they say that individuals matter. You matter. In fact, everything we do matters, because it affects those around us. Every type of project that human beings can envision—whether they be companies, capital funds, incubators, universities, or whatever—can be designed in ways to honor the best of human nature, to encourage the values that are conducive to innovation.

This new way of thinking about economic value is not just an academic curiosity. It is a moral responsibility to future generations. Real lives are at stake. Think of the wars started over lack of alternative fuels, the deaths caused by undrinkable water, the illnesses caused by drugs that were never commercialized, and the businesses failed because of structural silos.

This book by Henry and Alistair should be honored because it pushes the way forward. Not just for a select few, but for everyone. It is a path to a more sustainable and prosperous world, bringing new solutions for big challenges, new ventures to aging communities, and new sparks of life to revive great organizations.

That is why we are releasing this book under a Creative Commons license, so that the world can "remix, tweak, and build upon" this work non-commercially. We just ask that you credit the original book and license your work under the same terms.

The ideas in the *Rainforest Scorecard* seem simple at first. But don't be fooled. There is rigorous science that we've hidden away like the engine of a fine sports car. The Rainforest ideas draw from the latest research in complex systems theory, cognitive and behavioral sciences, evolutionary biology, legal studies, design thinking, political economy, and macrosociology.

Finally, remember that innovation culture has its own rules of engagement. It calls us to a different way of interacting with others. Handshakes, for instance, can be more binding than contracts. Altruism is often more efficient than selfishness. And silly things like trust and dreams and love—they really do power the world.

Victor W. Hwang
Los Altos, California
January 18, 2015

INTRODUCTION
*Henry Doss
& Alistair Brett*

The Rainforest Scorecard

The Rainforest Scorecard provides a strategy for creating economic value in the 21st century, by building and nurturing an innovative organizational culture. The scorecard, applied within the context of a carefully structured deployment process, functions as a modern framework for measuring and building culture at scale, in both public sector organizations and private businesses. It speaks to the key issues associated with deploying pragmatic strategies throughout an organization in order to develop innovation potential. We believe that the approach and framework outlined here is essential for fostering the growth of new products, services, and enterprises; for creating high-wage, knowledge-based jobs; and for enhancing sustainable economic competitiveness. We further believe that a highly innovative, efficient and trusting culture is the single most critical challenge in achieving these goals.

The Rainforest Scorecard is based on the notion that understanding, measuring and intentionally growing and developing an innovation culture is a deeply pragmatic exercise, aimed at pragmatic outcomes. The Scorecard supports this outcome by addressing those organizational and leadership issues associated with deploying working, measurable strategies into an organization, in an empirical and data-centric manner, with cultural improvements that can be tracked, reported and understood by leadership.

However, the use of the term "score" is not to be understood as placing inordinate value on assessment or scoring or evaluation per se; rather, the scorecard should serve as a means of establishing a baseline for ongoing organizational dialogue and a shared cultural narrative of innovation. The scorecard provides organizations an opportunity to institutionalize language, terms, ideas and thinking, as an outcome of the work involved in completing the evaluation, and to create a baseline measurement that can be used for looping feedback and progress measurement later. It is important to remember that these internal behavior and language steps are as important, if not more important, than the actual results of completing the scorecard. A too intense focus on scoring will diminish the returns possible by focusing on dialogue.

The scorecard does not provide any particular approach, process, method, or tool that serves as "an answer" or a pre-set, proscribed way of doing things with respect to innovation and organizational culture; instead, the process and scoring model seek to describe an ideal organizational "system state"—the aggregate set of conditions or features of systems that are generally present in innovative organizations. This idealized model is in turn used as a gauge against which organizations can measure and evaluate their own state of innovation. In execution, the scorecard fosters an in-depth, honest examination of an organization's culture, leadership approach, innovation resources/ assets, networks, and policies—the sum of which in operation constitute that organization's culture. The result of this process is the identification of opportunities to improve a culture's propensity toward innovation.

The Rainforest Master Plan

The Rainforest Scorecard is part of an overall implementation process we call *the Rainforest Master Plan (RaMP)*. The RaMP process is inspired by the impact of the *Malcolm Baldrige National Quality Award,* which the U.S. created in 1988 to foster and recognize organizational excellence. In ways similar to the Baldrige Award, RaMP guides organizations through structured, outcome-oriented conversations about innovation states, focusing on several key areas of assessment; these organizational conversations in turn support the creation of innovation ecosystems that make communities, organizations and businesses more resilient and sustainable.

The RaMP process, in conjunction with the Rainforest Scorecard, merges the science of innovation with a pragmatic business process to engineer innovation systems and cultures.

The RaMP and the Rainforest Scorecard together are:

> Grounded in science-based Rainforest innovation principles.
> Based on proven strategies for deployment, design and iterative discovery.
> Clearly defined practices and an empirical innovation scorecard that work as a:
>> Descriptor and template of innovative culture.
>> Guide to learning and organizational conversation.
>> Benchmark scoring device to gauge internal progress over time.

Working together, the RaMP and Rainforest Scorecard create:

> Evidence-centered processes that specifically target culture, leadership and resources;
> An empirical inquiry into leadership and the degree to which leadership supports innovation.
> A strategic framework that renders the subjective discussion of culture empirical.

Engaging the RaMP process and Rainforest Scorecard as an iterative program of work will produce:

> Systems and cultures that are firmly grounded in innovative principles and practices.
> Innovative networks and relationships, grounded in trust, which produce efficiency and productivity.
> More risk taking, trial, and iteration
> Increases in innovation, trust-based velocity, capacity building, and sustainability.

The Science of Innovation: The Roots of the Rainforest

Understanding and leading innovative cultures is an exercise in applying the science and principles of innovative cultures to the leadership of organizations. The following section provides a brief overview of the fundamental concepts that apply to Rainforest innovation systems, and a perspective on the core drivers of innovation ecosystems.

The Rainforest innovation model is science-based and is derived from contemporary research developments in complexity, biology, psychology, sociology, and other related disciplines. The Rainforest Scorecard and RaMP process synthesize these multiple disciplines of thought into a new understanding regarding sustainable economic development. This empirical approach allows organizations to tackle complex systems, intractable problems, and entrenched cultures across huge networks, using aligned languages and concepts.

The science of innovation requires an integrated mix of numerous components that work collectively to produce an ecosystem conducive to generating, capturing, and developing innovation wherever it may arise. Central to the Scorecard and RaMP process are the six categories of innovation that form its philosophical foundations. These categories address both cultural and structural issues and are:

LEADERSHIP

FRAMEWORKS, INFRASTRUCTURE, POLICIES

RESOURCES

ACTIVITIES, ENGAGEMENT

ROLE MODELS

CULTURE

These six categories are the focus of the Scorecard. In evaluating and scoring an organization's current state of innovation, each of the six categories is evaluated in two domains:

> Assets

> Human Resources

It is very important to understand the organizational and cultural distinction between assets and human resources, when seeking to understand an organization's capacity for innovation. In the Rainforest model, these two domains function similarly to hardware and software in computing systems.

ASSETS

There are four principal organizational assets in innovation systems: *People, Professions, Infrastructure and Policies.* These assets function like the hardware of a computing system: they tend to be fixed over time and are changed on a relatively slow scale. They are the "processing" part of the organization, responding to inputs and delivering output. Most organizations have some variation of all of these hardware components and this part of the system is what generally gets the most attention in organizational leadership—because it is the most visible.

HUMAN RESOURCES

The human resources features of an organization are: *Diversity, Extra-rational Motivations, Social Trust; Rules of the Rainforest;* and *Interpretation of Rules.* These elements function like the software of a computer system. They are the inputs, the instructions and the "code" that determine what the system can deliver. They tend to be complex, error-prone, and in need of constant adjustment and "updates"; they are often a bit mysterious, because they operate behind the scenes and are often misunderstood. And they often get the least attention.

Assets and human resources interact to produce innovation, but it is the natural tendency of organizations to focus on the asset side. This is because actions on the hardware side—the asset side—are more easily measured, seen, and displayed.

But these hardware assets are not worth very much without the software—the culture—piece. Absent trust, an incubator will not be very innovative. Absent willingness to fail, accelerator programs will not produce much acceleration. Absent the human resources elements that create innovative thinking and innovative dreaming, hardware investments are generally more show than substance.

There are several advantages to adopting this bipartite point of view— assets and human resources—of innovation:

First, doing so can help you to focus on the hard part of innovation: the human side. When innovation strategies are focused on the "asset" side of this model, the results can be minimal: fiddling around with job descriptions, creating new innovation policies, building innovation "spaces" and so on. While none of these are inherently counter to innovation, they are at best low-hanging fruit; at worst they distract time and energy from the real work of driving cultural change.

Second, by focusing more attention on the human resources side of the organizational equation, you might find yourself doing better strategic thinking about innovation. Adopting this framework gives you a shared organizational lexicon that can dramatically speed up thinking and planning. In every strategic conversation you can ask yourself: "Am I talking about assets or human resources?" And answering this question will help you determine if you're focusing on real change, or possibly less-important change.

Finally, this framework will ensure that culture—the most critical piece of innovation—is on everyone's agenda. Again, it's easy to get distracted from doing hard work on engineering an innovative culture, by succumbing to the allure of the less complex. Driving innovation is a matter of staying focused on culture changes — the human side of the equation.

Assets and human resources are mutually dependent, and the true innovation culture is one that is robust in both dimensions. This means that everyone is paying just as much attention to the human resources elements as they are to the more easily quantified asset elements.

Moving Forward

The completion of the Rainforest Scorecard is only the beginning of a long-term process leading to the development of a more innovative organization. The goal of this initial scoring process is to identify strengths and areas of improvement that may be promoted and developed in support of innovation. It is also meant to be a blueprint for how to proceed with the new information with regard to next steps. It is essential to recognize that there is no "right answer" or no "best score" in the assessment process. Innovation is not formulaic and there are no discretely proscribed steps that can be taken to improve any ecosystem. Working through this scorecard process will make it clear that developing an innovative environment is in itself an innovative process and should be driven by the same principles that were used to complete this assessment.

Finally, all organizations operate from inside a "Social Contract," whether that contract is articulated or merely implicit. As organizations work through this Rainforest Scorecard process, the following six principles, understood as a social contract to guide the work, may provide focus and clarity:

1. Learn by Doing
2. Make Social Contracts Explicit
3. Enhance Diversity
4. Celebrate Role Models and Peer Interaction
5. Build Communities of Trust
6. Create Social Feedback Loops

The Rainforest Scorecard, consistently deployed in an organization in a sustained, iterative manner, can support a robust improvement in innovation within organizations. We invite readers and those who choose to engage in this process to share questions, concerns, ideas and feedback.

Henry Doss
henry@t2vc.com

Alistair Brett
alistair@t2vc.com

t2vc.com

SHORT-FORM RAINFOREST SCORECARD

This short-form scorecard is provided as a tool for dialogue and discussion. It is intended to be completed by individuals or teams, on a rapid-fire basis. An individual might complete this short-form assessment and develop a point of view about an organization. Select team members might complete this short assessment as preparation to begin discussions about innovation. Or, it might be shared, completed and aggregated in more formal ways to serve as a beginning point for introducing Rainforest concepts into an organization. However it is used, it should be thought of as: 1) a quick, intuitive assessment of innovation conditions in an organization and 2) introductory in nature and intended to prepare for the more in-depth and intense work necessary to complete the comprehensive assessment.

INSTRUCTIONS FOR SCORING SELF-ASSESSMENT

The Organizational Profile section is not scored and is meant to be introductory. The sections following the Organizational Profile are scored on the basis of level of agreement with the statements listed. The scoring ranges for each section are described under each header.

Organizational Profile (not scored)

Who are the organization's leaders? *List as many as you can.*

Why are they leaders? Be specific.

Leadership (200 pts)

(0 = I don't know/disagree, 10 = moderately disagree, 20 = moderately agree, 30 = agree, 40 = strongly agree)

Leadership	Points
Overall, leadership promotes innovation. **(40 pts)**	
Leadership's perspective aligns with the perspective of others in the organization working to promote innovation. **(40 pts)**	
Leadership comes from diverse backgrounds and has diverse social, professional and cultural networks. **(40 pts)**	
Leaders are effective at communicating their visions and agendas to their constituencies. **(40 pts)**	
I understand the motivations of the organization's leadership. **(40 pts)**	

Section Total (200 max.) [   ]

Frameworks, Infrastructure, Policies (150 pts)

(0 = I don't know, 6 = disagree, 12 = moderately disagree, 18 = moderately agree, 24 = agree, 30 = strongly agree)

Frameworks, Infrastructure, Policies	Points
Stakeholders involved in innovation have strong communication channels and collaborations. **(30 pts)**	
I can identify and describe all of the steps of the innovation process and the key players. **(30 pts)**	
Organizational policies in general help potential innovators. **(30 pts)**	
There are effective mechanisms of feedback where different stakeholders can learn from each other. **(30 pts)**	
Communication infrastructure is robust and comparable to highly innovative organizations. **(30 pts)**	
Section Total (150 max.)	

Resources (150 pts)

(0 = I don't know, 6 = disagree, 12 = moderately disagree, 18 = moderately agree, 24 = agree, 30 = strongly agree)

Resources	Points
It is easy for innovators to access funding for their ventures. **(30 pts)**	
Up to date, relevant, and current information across a broad spectrum of disciplines is accessible by the majority of the organization. **(30 pts)**	
The organization's workforce is highly diverse and talented across a broad range of relevant skill sets that align with market demands. **30 pts)**	
There are effective entre- and/or intrapreneurial support organizations and individuals with experience that are available to mentor and support innovation. **(30 pts)**	
There are programs that specifically train workers to be current in their field and these programs are widely accessible. **(30 pts)**	
Section Total (150 max.)	

Activities and Engagement (100 pts)

(0= I don't know/disagree, 5=moderately disagree, 10=moderately agree, 15=agree, 20=strongly agree)

Activities and Engagement	Points
There are numerous (>10) organizational activities that actively promote innovation. **(20 pts)**	
These activities are effective in promoting innovation. **(20 pts)**	
These activities span a large spectrum of technical domains and promote collaboration across diverse audiences. **(20 pts)**	
These programs have a high degree of engagement among diverse groups of participants. **(20 pts)**	
There are effective means of developing new high engagement activities in the organization to promote innovation. **(20 pts)**	
Section Total (100 max.)	

Role Models (100 pts)

(0= I don't know/disagree, 5=moderately disagree, 10=moderately agree, 15=agree, 20=strongly agree)

Role Models	Points
Successful innovators are celebrated as role models in the organization. **(20 pts)**	
These role models are actively engaged in supporting innovation through a variety of means. **(20 pts)**	
These role models are widely known by the general public in the organization. **(20 pts)**	
Formal recognition is given for innovative contributions to the organization. **(20 pts)**	
There are systems to recognize and support high-potential future role models. **(20 pts)**	
Section Total (100 max.)	

Culture (300 pts)

(0= I don't know, 10=disagree, 20=moderately disagree, 30=moderately agree, 40=agree, 50=strongly agree)

Culture	Points
Trust is an important cultural element and is widespread and easily created. **(50 pts)**	
People think in terms of "positive-sum" or "win-win" situations and not "zero-sum" or "I win only if you lose" **(50 pts)**	
Failure is not viewed in a negative light. **(50 pts)**	
Calculated risk taking is viewed positively. **(50 pts)**	
People are often willing to help without expectation of immediate return. **(50 pts)**	
People are encouraged to dream and "think big". **(50 pts)**	
Section Total (300 max.)	

Total (out of 1000)	

THE
RAINFOREST
SCORECARD

Scoring Guidelines & Principles

SCORING

The Rainforest Scorecard provides a comprehensive evaluation of an organization's innovation potential. The scoring methodology is based on the notion that objective scoring is a necessary, initial step to begin the process of cultural change. The scale, scope and level of detail which may be reached in completing this process will vary from organization to organization, and is a function of available time and resources. However, irrespective of scale, all assessment efforts will follow certain guidelines, in order to optimize their return on the effort required to complete the scorecard.

HOW TO SCORE

It will be clear when working through the scorecard that many of the concepts are not very easy to measure. In contrast to more traditional measurements that are more apparent and accessible, many of the concepts of innovation are much more fluid. Cultural concepts such as trust, extra-rational motivations, and the impact of diverse networks, among others are often difficult to measure, and very likely, new means of measurement will emerge. Initially, the primary value of the scoring process lies in the recognition of the concepts and the thought processes intrinsic to innovation.

UNDERSTANDING THE MEANING OF "HOW"

In this document, there is often a requirement to determine "how." There are two forms of this question: one asks a method question, such as how is X measured?: the second asks a qualitative question, such as "How valuable is X?" For method questions, a detailed outline of any methods used to address the question should be presented. Such an outline would include processes, people involved, metrics used, and modes of evaluation. If there is no currently employed method, proposals for new methods of gathering adequate information should be explored or suggested as part of answering the question. The second question is much more subjective and ideally should be answered with data obtained across key organizational participants through surveys or other forms of data collection.

HONESTY AND INTEGRITY

The scorecard is only as valuable as the effort expended in using it. It is not designed to be proscriptive regarding what to do or how to do it; rather it serves to introduce a number of inquiries about concepts of highly innovative ecosystems. Many of the answers may not be immediately apparent and in some cases it may not even be clear how to go about discovering the answers. Often the best answer may be simply, "I don't know" and this is perfectly acceptable. Innovation is a continuously evolving, iterative process, and effective engagement with the scorecard requires a commitment to candor and transparency, in service to authentic inquiry.

UNDERSTANDING ASSETS AND HUMAN RESOURCES

For each of the six sections there are two principle subsections: *Assets* and *Human Resources*. These subsections are scored in different ways as outlined here.

Assets

SCORING CRITERIA

Asset scoring criteria are measured based on the following elements;

> Resource Access
> Communication/Collaboration
> Positive Incentives
> Feedback Mechanisms and Quality
> Network Quality
> Knowledge and Talent Quality

ASSET SCORING DOMAINS
(percentages of total possible score)

Asset scoring domains are based on a simple "low–high" metric. It is of note that not all sections dealing with assets will address all of the above six elements, in which case only elements addressed in the section should be considered to evaluate weighting. For example, a section on networks that does not address resource access, such as funding, should only evaluate the quality of the network element when evaluating the scoring weighting.

0–25%

Very little to zero resource access, collaboration between stakeholders, positive incentives, feedback mechanisms, network quality, or talent quality.

25–50%

Low-moderate quality levels of asset metrics. For example, asset elements that extend to only a few stakeholders such as resources accessible in only a few places or networks that include only specific small segments of the community.

50–75%

Moderate-high quality and distribution of asset elements based on inclusion and access.

75–100%

Nearly complete access and distribution of high quality resources across all stakeholders of a community. For example, open networks that have extensive and wide spread participation, high quality resources that are freely available to the entire community or feedback mechanisms that are comprehensive, robust, and engaging to all stakeholders.

Example of Asset Scoring Method:

Category:
Activities: Engagement

Evaluation:
Engagement in activities supporting innovation is strong, but limited to selected groups of individuals that are not highly diverse. Strong efforts are made to increase engagement across activities.

Scoring Domain:
50-75%

Total Points Available:
25

Score Assigned:
13-18

Human Resources

SCORING CRITERIA

The Human Resources scoring criterion is based on a spectrum that ranges from characteristics typical of "farm" economics to characteristics of "Rainforest" economics. The criteria listed below are qualitative measures of human resources tendencies. Each of the human resources criteria carries a numeric maximum value that is then weighted by a percentage as defined by the domain weighting based on the tendencies of each of the stakeholders involved in that particular section. For example, for sections relating to leadership, the maximum scores would be multiplied by a certain percentage based on the inclinations of leaders toward either farm or Rainforest characteristics. Not all of the criteria will apply in every case. Weighting percentages are based on both strength and breadth of tendencies across the criteria.

Farm Criteria	—	Rainforest Criteria
Central Planning	—	Decentralized Iteration
Zero-Sum Transactions	—	Positive Sum Transactions
Uniformity	—	Diversity
Rationally Selfish	—	Extra Rational Motivation
Conservative	—	Dreamer
Emphasize Certainty	—	Embrace Ambiguity
High Degrees of Formality	—	High Degrees of Trust
Silos of Activity	—	Extensive Promotion of Collaboration

HUMAN RESOURCES SCORING WEIGHTS
Multipliers of total score values for each subcategory of Culture

0–25%

All stakeholder tendencies (or subcategories) lean toward farm Mode. Very little evidence of Rainforest Mode characteristics

25–50%

Mix of stakeholder values (or subcategories) leaning toward Farm Mode. The mix may be within a single stakeholder group, such as a mix of "Rainforest" leaders mixed with "farm" leaders or may occur as a mix of stakeholder perspectives, such as a "Rainforest" university system and a "Farm" government.

50–75%

Mix of stakeholder values (or subcategories) leaning toward Rainforest Mode. Similar to criteria for 25–50% group but with greater Rainforest tendencies within or across stakeholder groups.

75–100%

Nearly complete Rainforest Mode characteristics across all innovation stakeholders (or subcategories)

Example of Human Resources Scoring Method:

Category:
Role Models: Recognition

Evaluation:
Recognition of accomplishments is not frequently given. Additionally, recognition tends to stress adherence to rules and regulations and does not emphasize characteristics such as collaboration and experimentation.

Scoring Domain:
0-25%

Total Points Available:
25

Score Assigned:
0-6

Describe the structural and strategic composition of your organization.

1.1 Who are the key stakeholders engaged in organizational innovation?

1.1.1   Entrepreneurs. Who are they? Where do they come from? Is there a general profile of an entrepreneur?

1.1.2   Universities, Knowledge Centers, and Educational/Training Centers. What are the sources of new knowledge in the organization?

1.1.3   Capital Sources. What are the various sources of capital for innovation in the organization? What are the entities that provide it? How accessible is capital for innovative ideas within the organization?

1.1.4   Innovation/Entrepreneurial Support Organizations. What are the key organizations that promote and support organizational innovation, both internal and external?

1.1.5   Major Industries and Commercial Entities. What customer/supplier relationships are most supportive of innovation? What are the major organizational industries or commercial entities that serve as partners? How are these distributed in the organization? Are there specific clusters?

1.1.6   Government. What are the departments of government that affect innovation? What is the general role of government in innovation, regional, local and Federal?

1.2 What are the key assets of the organization?

1.2.1   Physical Resources. What are the major physical resources available in the organization?

1.2.2   Intellectual Resources. What are the key intellectual resources of the organization?

1.2.3   Workforce. What is a general profile of the organizational workforce?

1.2.4   Infrastructure. What is the state of transportation and communication networks in the organization?

1.3 Describe the strategic position of your organization.

1.3.1 What are the principle industries or sectors that the organization participates in?

1.3.2 What is the organization's strategic position in the local economy? Regional Economy? Global economy?

1.4 Vision and Goals

1.4.1 What is the overall vision?

1.4.2 What sectors/industries are focal points for the vision and goals?

1.4.3 Are there non-economic goals for organizational development?

1.5 Goals

1.5.1 What measures and indicators are important to evaluate success?

1.5.2 What are the desired targets for these measures and indicators?

1.5.3 How will these measures and indicators be measured?

SECTION 2—LEADERSHIP (200 POINTS)

Identifying leaders and champions in the organization will be one of the most essential first steps in assessing innovative potential. Leaders of innovation must have a clear understanding of the motivations, experiences, and perspectives of their organization's potential, in order to better understand the decision-makers and influencers.

Who are your leaders and champions in each of the below arenas and what are their characteristics and effectiveness?

2.1 Assets	Points
2.1.1 Governance. Who are the key leaders in governance at different levels? What is the level of their support for an innovation-based organization? How do they publically convey this message? Who are the champions for innovation within the levels of governance? What is their role and influence in the organization? **(20 pts)**	
2.1.2 Workforce. Who are the key drivers of innovation in the organization (leaders/champions of innovation)? In what context do they work? What kind of influence do they have? **(20 pts)**	
2.1.3 Knowledge leaders. Who are the key thought leaders in research and development? What is their level of support for a knowledge-based innovation organization? How prominent are they in supporting new and breakthrough thinking that encourages innovation? **(20 pts)**	
2.1.4 Credibility. How credible are leaders with regards to their ability to lead the development of an innovative ecosystem? From where does this credibility arise? Education? Experience? Elsewhere? **(20 pts)**	
2.1.5 Communication. How effective are leaders at communicating their visions and messages to their constituencies? How effective are they at communicating vision to their peers? What steps do leaders take to ensure that their vision is clear to the public? And how is this clarity measured and discussed? **(20 pts)**	

Section 2.1 Assets Subtotal (100 max.)

2.2 Human Resources	Points

2.2.1 Experience. What kind of experience relative to innovation do leaders have? Do they have experience launching new ventures? Growing successful companies? Do they have varied cultural experiences which highly effective innovative ecosystems tend to have? **(20 pts)**

2.2.2 Nature and Scope of Vision. How visionary is leadership? What vision do leaders have for organizational innovation? How aligned are these visions across leaders with different roles in the organization? **(20 pts)**

2.2.3 Motivations. Can the motivations of leaders be evaluated? If so, how? To what degree do extra-rational motivations play a role in leadership actions? **(20 pts)**

2.2.4 Trust. To what degree are leaders trusted by their constituencies? How do they foster this trust? What is leadership's commitment to ethical behavior? **(20 pts)**

2.2.5 Diversity, Networks, and Openness. What is the degree of diversity among organizational leadership? Experience? Culture? Gender? How is diversity among leadership promoted? To what degree do leaders' networks span different boundaries? Social boundaries across different levels of social class? Professional boundaries across different disciplines and professionals? Cultural boundaries across different organizations and cultures? To what degree do leaders possess a keystone ablity? How open and accessible are leaders, in general? **(20 pts)**

Section 2.2 Human Resources Subtotal (100 max.)

Section 2 Total (200 max.)

SECTION 3—FRAMEWORKS, INFRASTRUCTURE, AND POLICIES (150 POINTS)

Frameworks, Infrastructure, and Policies form the structural landscape for organizational innovation. They include all the organizations, departments, support infrastructure, and policies that have a role in the process of innovation. This section is a process of identifying who these stakeholders are and the policies that determine their action and interaction.

What are the Organizational Frameworks, Infrastructures, and Policies and how do these impact innovation?

3.1 Assets	Points
3.1.1 Stakeholders and Policies. What is the function of each stakeholder? Do cross-functional stakeholders exist and if so what are they? How aware are different stakeholders of the activities of others? How much collaboration is there across stakeholders? How is this measured? What is the frequency of communication/collaboration? What are policies regarding communication/collaboration between stakeholders? **(20 pts)**	
3.1.2 Feedback Loops. What are the established feedback mechanisms with the various stakeholders of the organization? Who do they engage? Are they effective and how is this determined? How is feedback evaluated? Is there both upwards and downwards feedback? What is done with the results? **(20 pts)**	
3.1.3 Innovation Flow. Where do innovative ideas come from? What is their flow through the different stakeholders of the organization. What steps do they pass through? Who are the key personnel in this process? Are there positions that specifically facilitate this flow? Who are the formal and informal spanning personnel that serve to connect different stakeholders? What is their level of influence in the organization? **(20 pts)**	
3.1.4 Networks. What is the nature of networks in the organization? Are they formal networks? Informal networks? Who do they engage? How diverse are they? How active are they? How is their activity measured? How do these networks arise? Are they imposed from the top down or generated from the bottom up? To what degree are individuals encouraged to engage in different networks? Are there systems to promote and maintain weak links? **(20 pts)**	
3.1.5 Support Infrastructure. What are the infrastructure elements that support institutional innovation states? Communication infrastructure? Global, regional or local market links? In what way do these elements support innovation? Are there any infrastructure gaps in the innovation process? **(20 pts)**	

Section 3.1 Assets Subtotal (100 max.)

3.2 Human Resources	Points
3.2.1 Trust. How formal are interactions between different stakeholders and within stakeholder groups? How much paperwork is involved? What is the degree of transparency of operations within each stakeholder? How is transparency determined and what efforts serve to increase transparency? To what degree are the activities of different stakeholders trusted by others? Are there key bottlenecks where lack of trust or transparency hinders the innovation process? **(25 pts)**	
3.2.2 Incentives/Motivations. How do policies affect incentives and motivations for stakeholders and stakeholder interactions? Do policies promote communication and collaboration both within and between stakeholders? Are policies controlling or enabling for stakeholders? Do policies provide disincentives to contribute to the innovation process? **(25 pts)**	

Section 3.2 Human Resources Subtotal (50 max.)

Section 3 Total (150 max.)

SECTION 4—RESOURCES (150 POINTS)

Resources form the foundation for both the generation and implementation of innovation. Physical resources are an essential element of the implementation of innovation; knowledge resources are essential for the generation of innovative ideas; and human resources span both functions. Understanding the quantity, quality, and origins of the array of resources available to an organization provides a fundamental understanding of its innovative potential.

What resources are available to support innovative initiatives and how accessible are they to innovators?

4.1 Assets	Points

4.1.1 Funding. What are the sources of funding for new, innovative ideas? How much is available from each source? How much emphasis is placed on ensuring the predictability and sustainability of this funding? How accessible is this funding? What are the policies regarding the allocation of this funding source and by type of the allocation of funding? How is the effectiveness of funding evaluated? What activities need funding to support them? **(20 pts)**

4.1.2 Knowledge. Where do innovative ideas originate? What forms of support go towards these sources of innovative ideas? How effective is this support? What are the knowledge-based resources available to innovators such as access to publications/databases, R&D, patents, etc.? How are the outputs and ideas in R&D made available to interested individuals? How is R&D viewed within the organization: Critical? Important? Unknown? How are relations between research providers, and other areas of the organization? Are brokers available to help match R&D needs to sources? **(20 pts)**

4.1.3 People. Who are the key innovative people in the organization? In what ways are these people encouraged and supported? How are they engaged in the innovative organization? Who are innovative role models? What is the depth of experience of leaders who serve as role models and mentors? **(20 pts)**

4.1.4 Support Organizations and Service Providers. Are there specific departments/ organizations or initiatives that support innovation in the organization? How extensive/diverse are their resource capabilities? Is there access to domain expertise? How is the effectiveness of these organizations measured? How developed are the industries or service providers that assist innovators, such as legal, financial, regulatory, human resources, etc.? How does the state of these support industries compare to organizational peers? What metrics can be used to make this comparison? **(20 pts)**

4.1.5 Talent. How talented is the labor pool? What is the educational/skill profile of the workforce population? How does it match with market demands, particularly in advanced-technology and knowledge sectors? What programs exist for organizational workforce development in a variety of skills including technical and entrepreneurial education? **(20 pts)**

Section 4.1 Assets Subtotal (100 max.)

4.2 Human Resources	Points

4.2.1 Funding and Support. To what degree do sources of funding and support promote "big thinking"? To what degree do policies regarding resource allocation promote experimentation and risk-taking? Are innovators dis-incentivized from experimentation for fear of losing funding? Are there funds allocated specifically for exploratory projects? Are there funds allocated specifically for cross-disciplinary or diverse teams or projects? **(25 pts)**

4.2.2 Motivations. For people, role models, support organizations, and service providers identified above, to what extent are they motivated by extra-rational motivations to provide resources back to the organization? How extensive is the participation in mentoring to support innovation and risk-taking? How open are individuals and organizations to sharing advice, support, and resources with new entrepreneurs? Are service providers and support organizations willing to share risk with entrepreneurs, for example by delaying fees for services or offering support for free? To what extent is the organization willing to defer immediate returns for long term gain? **(25 pts)**

Section 4.2 Human Resources Subtotal (50 max.)

Section 4 Total (150 max.)

SECTION 5—ACTIVITIES AND ENGAGEMENT (100 POINTS)

Activities and engagement represent a measure of the vibrancy of an organizational economy. Activities that are initiated on an organizational level (i.e. top down) are an important signal to constituencies of organizational ambition and commitment to innovation. Activities that promote innovation and actively encourage engagement across a diverse array of participants are an essential part of a thriving innovative ecosystem.

What programs/activities are in place to promote innovation and how is engagement in these initiatives encouraged?

5.1 Assets	Points
5.1.1 Activities. What are the principle organizational activities that are currently in place to encourage innovation? What is the focus of these initiatives? Challenges? Collaborations? Tournaments? Etc.? What topics do they address in general? How is the success of these programs determined? What are the mechanisms for developing new programs and activities and who are the key players that are part of this process? What are the guiding principles that mold the development of new programs and activities? What are the goals of such activities? **(25 pts)**	
5.1.2 Engagement. What is the degree of engagement in activities that promote innovation? Who are the key people that are most engaged? How is this engagement measured? What efforts are in place to improve engagement both internal and external? How is the success of these efforts measured? What initiatives are in place to enhance engagement and/or recruit new participants? Are there structural barriers to enhancing engagement and, if so, what are they? **(25 pts)**	

Section 5.1 Assets Subtotal (100 max.)

5.2 Human Resources	Points
5.2.1 Thinking Big and Experimentation. What is the scope of activities to promote innovation? Do they encourage big, ambitious thinking? On what scale? To what degree do activities promote experimentation and iteration? **(25 pts)**	
5.2.2 Diversity and Motivations. To what degree do activities encourage diversity across a spectrum of characteristics such as age, background, experience, knowledge, culture, and technical domain? To what degree is collaboration a key element in activities? Are the motivations/reasons of engaged individuals understood? Have these motivations been incorporated into new activities? Are there incentives to be more engaged in innovative activities? Are there disincentives? **(25 pts)**	

Section 5.2 Human Resources Subtotal (50 max.)

Section 5 Total (100 max.)

SECTION 6—ROLE MODELS (100 POINTS)

Role models come in all shapes and sizes and are those individuals who embody characteristics that others wish to emulate. They are powerful influencers for the accelerated learning of new social behaviors and can transform entire organizations through inspiration.

What are the key success stories of the past and present and how are the champions of those stories highlighted?

6.1 Assets	Points
6.1.1 **People.** What have been the major innovative milestones accomplished in the organization and who have been the key individuals responsible? What role do these people currently play in the organization? How engaged are they in organizational activities/development that promote innovation? Who are the key people that will be the future innovators in the organization? How are they supported? Who are prominent role models outside of the organization? **(50 pts)**	

Section 6.1 Assets Subtotal (50 max.)

6.2 Human Resources	Points
6.2.2 Perception and Motivation. How well known are role models throughout the organization? What is the general perception of innovative people in the organization? Outside of the organization? How is this perception determined? Why are role models engaged in the organization? What is the nature of their extra-rational motivations? **(25 pts)**	
6.2.2 Recognition. What are mechanisms of recognition in the organization? How do these compare to recognition mechanisms elsewhere? Is recognition sufficient? What characteristics does this recognition highlight? How frequent is recognition given and on what scale? Individual? Organizational? Industry? **(25 pts)**	

Section 6.2 Human Resources Subtotal (50 max.)

Section 6 Total (100 max.)

SECTION 7—CULTURE (300 POINTS)

Culture is the foundation for any innovative ecosystem and while it is a component of all other areas being evaluated, must be considered as an independent and isolated factor as well. The principles of shared culture will ultimately determine the success of any innovative initiatives.

What are the defining attributes of the organizational culture and how do they promote an innovative environment?

7.1 Assets	Points
7.1.1 **People.** What are the cultural backgrounds of the organization's leaders and how does this experience translate to the current organization? How strong is the cultural alignment of organizational stakeholders? How is this evaluated? **(100 pts)**	
Section 7.1 Assets Subtotal (100 max.)	

7.2 Human Resources	Points
7.2.1 Rules of the rainforest. *To what degree are the following culturlal norms present in the organization?*	
7.2.1.1 Break the rules and dream. What is the perception of "blue sky" thinking and non-conformists? **(20 pts)**	
7.2.1.2 Open doors and listen. To what degree are people accessible, both personally and professionally? **(20 pts)**	
7.2.1.3 Trust and be trusted. How important is both professional and social trust in the organization and how is it created? **(20 pts)**	
7.2.1.4 Experiment and iterate together. What is the extent of collaboration and iteration in the development of new products and services? **(20 pts)**	
7.2.1.5 Seek fairness over advantage. To what degree is fairness in interactions and "positive-sum" mentality exemplified? **(20 pts)**	
7.2.1.6 Err, fail, and persist. What is the cultural perception of failure? What are the social and professional costs of failure? What is the perception of risk takers? **(20 pts)**	
7.2.1.7 Pay it forward. To what degree will individuals provide assistance without immediate expectation of return? **(20 pts)**	
7.2.2 Diversity. What is the emphasis on the value of diversity? How is diversity promoted across numerous barriers? Social, Professional, Cultural? **(30 pts)**	
7.2.3 Motivations. What is the role of extra-rational motivations in the general culture? To what degree are these motivations understood and accepted? **(30 pts)**	

Section 7.2 Human Resources Subtotal (200 max.)

Section 7 Total (100 max.)

ABOUT THE AUTHORS

Henry H. Doss

Henry H. Doss has over thirty years of business experience in banking and venture capital, as well as life-long work in non-profits as a volunteer. His primary business background is in the financial services area, with a concentration in sales leadership, sales automation, data mining, TQM and consumer research. He currently serves as Chief Strategy Officer with T2 Venture Creation, a Silicon Valley-based venture capital firm. Henry's work is primarily in the area of innovation ecosystem consulting, the merger of theory and practice in innovation culture work and the study of innovation leadership. In particular he focuses on the correlations between culture and performance in organizations and has an abiding interest in how individuals grow and learn.

As a volunteer, Henry currently serves as the Executive in Residence for the College of Liberal Arts and Sciences at UNC – Charlotte. In this role he coaches and mentor students, contributes to curriculum improvements, works to expand the global reach of International Studies, and supports faculty in special projects. He has also served his community in other roles: UNC – Charlotte: Dean's Advisory Council and Past President, Alumni Board of Governors; Habitat for Humanity; Hospice; Olivet College (Trustee); The Charlotte, NC, Chamber of Commerce; The United Negro College Fund; Project Head Start; Board Chair, The National Committee for the New River; Board Member and 2nd Vice Chair, AdvantageWest (The Western North Carolina Regional Economic Development Commission).

Henry writes extensively on innovation, the impact of humanities studies on personal growth and leadership. He is a contributor to Forbes, and his blog can be read at: http://blogs.forbes.com/henrydoss/. In his spare time, he is a musician/singer-songwriter.

Alistair M. Brett

Alistair M. Brett has over thirty years of international consulting experience in developed and developing countries around the globe, as well as some 12 years in college teaching. He specializes in commercializing science and technology, and developing support mechanisms for technology commercialization, primarily for universities and research centers.

He has served on the Advisory Board of the (US) Federal Laboratory Consortium for Technology Transfer and was the co-founder of the Center for Technology Commercialization and the Center's graduate technology management degree programs at the Academy of National Economy in Moscow. In addition to his work in economic development, Alistair has over twenty years of experience in higher education administration.

With T2 Venture Creation, Alistair focuses on how understanding innovation ecosystems as complex adaptive systems not only opens up the large volume of research on such systems, but also helps to analyze, design, create, and maintain support for innovation in businesses, organizations, regions, and countries.

Alistair also serves as a senior consultant to The World Bank. His other consulting clients include: Oxford Innovation Ltd, USAID, Russian Academy of Sciences, AEA Technology plc, European Union, and CRDF, among others. He holds a B.Sc. in Physics from the University of London, and a Ph.D. in Physics, from the University of St. Andrews (Scotland), and Drexel University (USA).

Notes

Notes

Notes

Made in the USA
San Bernardino, CA
04 December 2018